Everybody Eats Tortillas

Everybody Eats Tortillas

Dolly Calderon Wiseman

To the Henry Boys! Cooking is fun! Dolly Wiseman

iUniverse, Inc.

New York Lincoln Shanghai

Everybody Eats Tortillas

iUniverse books may be ordered through booksellers or by contacting:

iUniverse
2021 Pine Lake Road, Suite 100
Lincoln, NE 68512
www.iuniverse.com
1-800-Authors (1-800-288-4677)

Cover design by Brandon Boyd, musician, artist and Dolly's son

Front cover photo is of Bianca Velasco.

ISBN-13: 978-0-595-39001-4 (pbk)
ISBN-13: 978-0-595-83392-4 (ebk)
ISBN-10: 0-595-39001-3 (pbk)
ISBN-10: 0-595-83392-6 (ebk)

Printed in the United States of America

Kids Are Cooks Cookbooks Series

To my mother, Priscilla Calderon, who traded a dozen homemade flour tortillas for her Norwegian friend's one dozen homemade *lefse*. On that day, I began to appreciate my heritage. I learned that families, who lived countries—or even continents—away, were enjoying food wrapped up in a tortilla, just as my family did.

Contents

Acknowledgments

Many people and events influenced my decision to write this book. My thanks go first to my parents, Isaac and Priscilla Calderon, who fostered my love of cooking. Second, many thanks go to BJ Diaferia, who told me for years that I had a cookbook inside of me. Thanks to my children, Darren, Brandon, and Jason Boyd, and Seth and Melissa Wiseman, who always eat my concoctions, and thanks also to Victoria Giraud, whose editorial suggestions and encouragement helped along the way. And lastly, a big *thank you* goes to my wonderful husband, Brad, for encouraging me and accompanying me in the kitchen during our exciting cooking adventures.

Everybody Eats Tortillas

Maria was excited and nervous as she dressed for school on a very cold January morning. She smiled as she pulled her new pink and white sweater over her head and stepped into her new blue jeans. Next, she checked her reflection in her dresser mirror to make sure she hadn't mussed her long, dark brown braids. Maria had to look her best because it was her first day in the third-grade at McKinley Elementary School.

Maria's father had just moved the family to Englewood, Colorado, over the winter holidays because of his new job. For Maria, everything seemed so different from her old home in San Diego, California. She felt homesick for her friends, her old neighborhood, and the sunny, warm Southern California weather. As she slipped on her warm boots, she remembered a day several months ago at her old school when a new girl had come into the class and was so scared that she had to go to the nurse's office. Maria wished that she had been friendlier to the new girl now that she herself was going to be the new girl at school.

But when she came into the kitchen that morning, she got really nervous. Maria saw that her grandmother had lovingly packed her lunchbox with a burrito. Grandma had taken one of her delicious homemade tortillas and stuffed it with last night's leftovers of meat and beans. She had wrapped it in foil to keep it warm and had placed it in Maria's lunchbox.

Maria sadly looked at her lunchbox next to the bowl of cereal in front of her. She didn't feel like eating.

"Eat your breakfast quickly, sweetheart. The school bus will be here any minute!" her mother warned.

Oh no! Why couldn't Grandma have packed a sandwich in my lunch for this first day of school? Maria thought.

"Are you worried about your first day at school, Maria?" her mother asked as she arranged the bows at the ends of Maria's braids. "It's a good thing that we went to your school on Saturday to find your classroom. Now try to eat something."

"Thank you, Mama," Maria said. Nervous thoughts began to race in her mind. *Do the kids in my class eat tortillas? Do they even know what tortillas are? They don't know me. Will they make fun of me? At least Grandma packed me an apple and cookies!*

Before Maria could express her fears, she heard the *toot-toot* of the school bus waiting at the corner. Maria quickly kissed her mother and grandmother good-bye and grabbed her coat.

"Adios!" she said as she dashed out the door.

"Don't forget your lunch!" Grandma called out as she held the lunchbox high in the air and ran after Maria.

"Thank you! Bye-bye!" Maria answered. She grabbed her lunchbox, sloshed through the melting snow on the sidewalk, and boarded the full and noisy bus.

Maria saw an empty seat next to a blonde-haired girl who looked about her own age. Maria smiled shyly and sat down.

"Hi! Are you new on this bus?" The girl smiled, showing her braces.

"Yes, we just moved here from San Diego," Maria answered.

"I've never moved before. I've been here since I was a baby. My name is Melanie. What's yours?" Melanie asked.

"My name is Maria. Do you like the school here?" Maria asked, hoping that she could find out something about her new school before she got there.

"Oh, sure," Melanie answered. "I've had my same friends since kindergarten, and we all like the same things, like my lunchbox. See?" Melanie held it up to show Maria. "We all made sure our moms bought the same lunchboxes so that we could all be alike," she said as she looked proudly at the pink and yellow flowered design on the front. "So I like school, I guess. Are you in Mr. Boyd's class?"

"No, I have Mrs. Ross," Maria said a little sadly, trying to cover up her lunchbox, as it had a picture of kittens playing on the front.

Maria's thoughts began to race.

Everyone likes the same things. I'm not like Melanie. I don't have blonde hair. I don't have braces. I don't have Mr. Boyd for a teacher. And now I know I can't open my lunchbox at this new school! Maybe I should just leave my lunchbox on the bus. No, if someone finds it, they'll probably just bring it to me in front of everyone in the class!

"We're here! Bye, see you later!" Melanie announced as the bus stopped at the school. Everyone stepped off the bus and began walking or running in different directions.

Maria felt shy at first. Her teacher, Mrs. Ross, was warm and friendly, and she introduced Maria to the classroom full of children.

Her new class was studying many of the same subjects she had learned about in her previous school. That should have made Maria happy, but she kept worrying about her lunchbox. In no time it was noon, and Mrs. Ross was dismissing the class for lunch.

"Maria, won't you come and sit with us?" Erin asked as the boys and girls headed to the cafeteria. She was a petite Asian girl and one of the friendly kids who had said hi when Maria first approached the classroom. Erin lifted her sack lunch and looked inside. "I guess I have a peanut butter and jelly sandwich again, like everyone else." She laughed.

"I can't sit with you!" Maria blurted out. "I...um...I think I have to go to the attendance office. But thanks anyway!" She turned and started toward the school offices to hide somewhere until she saw Mrs. Ross walking toward her. Maria sat alone at a corner table in the cafeteria and opened her lunchbox to quickly grab the apple.

She could smell the delicious burrito inside. She was really hungry now, but she wasn't brave enough to bring it out.

"Excuse me, Maria, but why aren't you eating with the girls from our class? Didn't they ask you to sit with them?" Mrs. Ross looked concerned.

"Yes, but—" Maria's face began to get red.

"What is it, Maria?" Mrs. Ross asked gently as she put her arm around Maria's shoulders.

"I'm embarrassed. It's the food I brought for lunch. The kids might think I'm strange because I don't have a peanut butter sandwich for lunch like they do."

"Well, let's see what you *do* have in your lunch, and I promise I won't think you're strange," Mrs. Ross whispered to Maria. When Maria opened her lunchbox and peeled back the foil wrapper, the wonderful aroma of the burrito made Mrs. Ross grin.

"I know what this is! You have a burrito made from a tortilla and filled with something that smells delicious! Who made this for you?"

"My grandmother always makes these for us," answered Maria with a little smile. "She's from Mexico."

"I know someone else who will make you feel better about your lunch," assured Mrs. Ross. "Do you mind if I call Dylan over here? She's the girl who sits next to you in class."

Maria reluctantly nodded her head yes.

"Dylan," Mrs. Ross called out, "can you come here and tell me what Maria has in her lunchbox?"

Dylan ran over and peeked in. "That's *lefse*! We eat those in my home!"

Not wanting to miss anything interesting, Erin rushed over to see what they were talking about.

"Oh! You have rice paper wraps in your lunch! Aren't they delicious?" she asked.

"You see, Maria," laughed Mrs. Ross, "many children of different cultures have similar bread, just like your tortillas. They just have different names for them. Why don't you eat your burrito now? After lunch, we'll see who else in our classroom eats tortillas."

Maria grinned at her teacher. She picked up her delicious burrito and ate it hungrily.

After lunch, as soon as the classroom of noisy children had settled down, Mrs. Ross drew a picture of a flat round tortilla on the board with her chalk. Next to it, she drew a picture of a rolled up tortilla. She turned to the class and said, "Our new student, Maria, had something like this in her lunch today. Dylan and Erin both knew what it was. Can anyone else tell me what this is?"

Melissa shyly raised her hand and said, "That looks like Chinese pancakes. We fill them with meat and vegetables for my favorite dinner called *mushu.*"

"Where is your family from, Melissa?" asked Mrs. Ross.

"Both of my parents were born in Beijing, China," Melissa said with a big smile.

"Good! Erin, where does your family come from?" asked Mrs. Ross.

"We are from Vietnam," Erin answered.

"And Dylan, where do your relatives come from?"

"My grandmother was born in Norway. We wrap our *lefse* around meat or cheese. I also like them for breakfast with butter and jam on the top and then rolled up!"

"Class, Maria calls her bread tortillas. Her family is from Mexico—" began Mrs. Ross.

Jason couldn't wait any longer. He felt like he was being ignored and wanted to play this game too.

"Mrs. Ross! My mom makes an Italian bread that looks just like tortillas. We call it *piadine!*"

"Thank you, Jason," laughed Mrs. Ross. "Anyone else?"

"We eat *lavash!*" piped in Tina. "We're Armenian, and we wrap our food, too, just like Maria did with her lunch."

"Thank you, Tina! Darren, do you eat tortillas?" asked Mrs. Ross.

"Yes, but sometimes my family likes to use blue corn flour to make our blue corn tortillas," answered Darren. "We are Native Americans, and we eat some of the same kind of foods that Maria does."

"I have relatives from Greece," exclaimed Vanessa. "We eat *pita*, and we wrap our food with it too!"

"They make Bedouin barley bread in Jordan," added Brandon. "I know, because my mom makes it, and it looks like those tortillas. We eat it with yogurt cheese balls."

"I know that in India they eat *chapatis*," volunteered David. "We had it at an Indian restaurant. We used *chapatis* to wrap around the delicious food we ate there."

"In Israel, they eat a round flatbread called *matzo*. We eat it soft or let it dry out and eat it like a cracker," added Seth. "We always have it at special holiday meals."

"My goodness!" exclaimed Mrs. Ross. "Look at all of the breads that are just like tortillas! Let's make tonight's homework a fun project. Let's all bring in the recipes for these breads tomorrow, and we'll make them in class later this week. If anyone finds out about other tortilla-like breads, bring in those recipes, too."

That night, Maria was excited as she told her family about her first day at school.

"So many of the children in my class eat tortillas," she explained, "but they call them different names. These tortillas are from countries all over the world." Then suddenly Maria had a great idea!

"Grandma, can you please teach me to make tortillas tonight? I want to share them with my friends at school tomorrow," Maria said with a big smile.

"I would be happy to!" her grandmother chuckled. "After you finish your homework, I will teach you how to make delicious tortillas the way our family has been preparing them for many, many years."

Maria realized that she was proud to eat tortillas.

Won't it be fun to learn how the other tortilla-like breads are made and how they are eaten? This new school is going to be interesting!

The next morning, Mrs. Ross happily collected twenty-two recipes from a very excited classroom.

"Class, you all did your homework and brought in so many wonderful recipes for flatbreads like tortillas! Our discussion about tortillas got me interested in the history of bread. I also did some homework and brought some information that will explain how people all over the world began eating bread. Did you know that thousands of years ago people ground wild grain on rocks to make flour? Then they put that flour in a bowl and added water. They mixed it all up with their hands and cooked their tortilla-like bread on hot flat rocks that they had heated in a fire pit. They didn't use utensils as we do today. A piece of flatbread made a perfect spoon, which they used to scoop up their food."

Mrs. Ross pulled down the big map of the world and pointed.

"Here is where Egypt is. The ancient Egyptians learned to make yeast bread around 2600 BC. They called it *aiysh*, their word for life. They lived near the Nile River that flooded every year and nourished the grain plants. When they harvested these plants, they would grind the seeds into flour. They were the first culture to eat bread that puffed up and was baked in stone ovens."

She pointed to the country of Greece on the map and continued. "The ancient Greeks learned bread-making from the Egyptians. The Greeks then taught the ancient Romans how to make bread. Since then, wheat, and bread made from wheat, has become the most important food for more than one-third of the world's people. I also read that the ancient Mayas of Mexico invented tortillas for a king over 10,000 years ago!" She pointed to Mexico on the map.

Maria shyly raised her hand.

"Yes, Maria?"

"Last night, I read that the Aztecs of ancient Mexico made thin cornmeal breads and called them *tlaxcalli*. When the Spanish explorers came to Mexico, they changed the word to *tortilla*, and they have been called that ever since. Last night, my grandmother taught me to make flour tortillas, and I brought some to share with the class. Would that be all right?" Maria asked.

"How nice of you to bring us a treat! Thank you, Maria," answered Mrs. Ross. "When we make everyone's flatbread recipes over the next few weeks, we will study where each country is on the world map. You will see that people are alike, not only here in our classroom, but in our city, in our country, and all over the world! These cooking lessons will be part of our geography studies. I know you will agree that Maria's tortillas make learning geography fun."

At lunchtime, Maria's classmates crowded together to share Maria's tortillas. While they ate their lunches, they talked excitedly about their recipes.

It will be fun to find out what else we have in common each day here in my new city! One thing I do know is that everybody eats tortillas! Maria thought happily as she ate the burrito she'd made for her lunch.

BEFORE YOU BEGIN COOKING FLATBREADS

Above: These are the most common cooking utensils used in tortilla preparation.

Kitchen Tools Needed to Make Flatbreads

It is important to remember that before doing any cooking, always have everything you will need near your cooking area. For most of these recipes, you will need the following:

1. Mixing bowls: Have a bowl the size of a cereal bowl and two more in larger sizes, about an 8-cup capacity.

2. Liquid measuring cups: These cups are clear pitchers with measuring markings on the side. To measure accurately, you need to look at your measurement from the side.

3. Dry measuring cups: These cups are made of plastic or metal and have a handle. When measuring dry ingredients such as flour, spoon the dry flour into the measuring cup and level it off with the handle of a wooden spoon to get an exact measurement.

4. Measuring spoons: These spoons measure from 1/4 teaspoon to 1 tablespoon.

5. A wooden spoon: This is a good tool to use to mix your flour and liquids before you use your hands to knead the dough.

6. A nonstick skillet: A 12-inch skillet is large and has a center that measures about 9 inches, perfect for tortilla making. A smaller 10-inch skillet has a center that measures 7 inches and is good for the recipes that require you to pour a batter in for a large pancake type of flatbread. If you don't have nonstick skillets, then you will have to oil the skillet periodically to keep your breads from sticking to the pan. When heating your skillet, start on a medium-high setting. To know when your skillet is the right temperature, sprinkle a few drops of water on it. If they dry up immediately, the pan is too hot. If they dance on the skillet, you are ready to cook. You may discover that you can reduce the heat to medium after you have cooked a few tortillas.

7. A spatula: Make sure that the head of the spatula is wide enough to help you turn a tortilla.

8. A rolling pin: When rolling out your dough, press the rolling pin in the center of the dough ball and roll away from you. Turn your flat-

tened piece of dough over to the back side, turn it 1/4 around, and roll it out again. Repeat this process until your tortilla has a nice round shape and is the size you want. To keep your bread in a circular shape, you may have to roll in a "C" direction. If you practice, you will have perfect tortillas every time. If your dough sticks to the rolling pin, spread some dry flour on it, and it will be easier to work with. (A note about tortilla presses: Many regular tortilla chefs find that this device makes constructing tortillas much easier. It looks like two heavy metal plates hinged together with an arm that presses down on the top plate. You simply place your ball of dough between the plates and press the top down to result in perfectly round bread every time. Flatbreads are much easier to roll out to a larger size after using this device.)

9. A breadboard: This board is usually wooden or plastic and used as a flat surface for chopping and preparing food. Most of the recipes call for a *floured breadboard*. This just means that you should sprinkle a handful of flour on the board and spread it with your hands. This keeps the dough from sticking to the board.

10. A wire whisk: This kitchen utensil is great for mixing eggs and other liquids.

11. A ruler: Because the recipes call for different sizes for the flatbreads you are making, have a ruler handy to measure their sizes.

12. A Ping-Pong ball, a golf ball, and a walnut: These are the approximate sizes described to roll out your dough balls.

More Important Cooking Tips

On the following pages are the flatbread recipes that Mrs. Ross's class brought to share. The recipes are not difficult to make. Cooking is easy! My mother always told me, "If you can read, you can cook." But please follow these few simple rules when you begin making any of these recipes:

1. Do not wear long-sleeve shirts. The sleeves might get in your way as you prepare food, or they might ignite when you are near an open flame.

2. If you have long hair, tie it back. It is easier to cook if your hair is out of your face. Besides, no one wants a stray hair in their food!

3. Have an adult nearby when you are using hot items like skillets and cookie sheets needed for these recipes.

4. Most of the recipes ask you to *knead* the dough. Kneading is done by pressing the heels of your hands into the center of the dough ball. Continue pressing outward until your hands are at the edge of the dough. Fold the dough back into the ball, turn it 1/4 turn, and knead again. Your hands will tell you when it is kneaded enough, when the dough ball has a smooth surface.

5. Follow the recipes exactly the first time to make sure your food will taste good.

6. *Always* remember to begin your cooking projects with clean hands!

If you have a family recipe for a tortilla-like flatbread that is not found here, please send it to me at www.KidsAreCooks.com. Enjoy these recipes, and remember that everybody eats tortillas!

Above: A plate of cooked tortillas

FLATBREAD RECIPES

Mrs. Ross's Ancient Egyptian Bread

You will need a mixing bowl, measuring spoons, liquid and dry measuring cups, a spatula, and a skillet.

In the mixing bowl, combine:

2 cups whole wheat flour
1 teaspoon salt
1 cup water

Knead the dough until the water is completely mixed into the flour.

Pull off walnut-sized pieces of the dough, roll them into balls, and flatten them into round disks with your hands. Make them as flat as possible. They will be about the size of a pancake.

Lay the flattened pieces of dough two at a time on a hot skillet until the bottoms get brown spots (about 30 seconds). Carefully flip them over with your spatula and cook for another 30 seconds. Repeat with the remaining flatbreads.

This recipe makes approximately 12 breads. Because this bread is made of whole wheat, it is rather dry. It's no wonder that the ancient Egyptians often used this flatbread as a spoon to scoop up a mouthwatering mixture of chopped dates, cinnamon, honey, and sesame seeds.

Maria's Flour Tortillas from Mexico

You will need a mixing bowl, measuring spoons, liquid and dry measuring cups, a wooden spoon, a floured breadboard, a rolling pin, a spatula, and a skillet.

In the mixing bowl, combine:

3-1/2 cups unbleached white flour

1 teaspoon salt

2 teaspoons baking powder

1/2 cup vegetable oil

1 cup warm water added slowly (Maria's great-grandmother often used 1/2 cup milk and 1/2 cup water)

Sprinkle a small amount of flour all over the breadboard.

Use your wooden spoon to mix the ingredients for the dough in the bowl. When it begins to stick together, mix it with your hands. When you have a slightly firm ball of dough, turn it onto the breadboard.

Knead the dough on the floured board until it is thoroughly mixed. Put it back into the bowl and let it rest for 15 minutes.

Tear off a piece of dough about the size of a Ping-Pong ball and roll it into a perfect ball.

Lay the piece of dough on the floured breadboard. Using a rolling pin, roll your piece of dough out so it makes a circle about 8 inches in diameter. Continue rolling out 8 balls of dough.

Heat up your skillet. Put your tortilla in the hot skillet to cook for about 30 seconds, or until it has brown freckles. When you see air bubbles in the tortilla, press them down with the spatula or a soft towel. Carefully turn the tortilla over with your spatula and cook another 45 seconds.

This recipe will make approximately 8 tortillas. Wrap them in a clean towel to keep them warm. They are delicious alone or wrapped around cheese, meat, or beans, and even spread with peanut butter and jelly!

Maria's Corn Tortillas from Mexico

For this recipe, you will need a mixing bowl, liquid and dry measuring cups, measuring spoons, a floured breadboard, a rolling pin, plastic wrap, a spatula, and a skillet.

In the mixing bowl, combine:

2 cups masa harina (also known as corn flour)
1-1/3 cups water
Optional ingredients:
1 teaspoon salt (for taste)
1 tablespoon corn oil (to make the tortillas easier to work with)

Mix the ingredients for the dough with your hands until you get a firm ball. (The optional ingredients above make the dough more flavorful and easier to work with.) Pull off a walnut-size ball and pat it between your hands until you get a 4-inch-round circle.

Place your small circle of dough between 2 pieces of plastic wrap. Roll the dough out with a rolling pin until it is bigger, about 6 inches in diameter. It is natural for the edges to look frayed and uneven. If you would like a smooth-edged tortilla, simply fold the rough edges back in to the tortilla, or cut them off with a knife in a circular direction.

Cook on a skillet for about 1 minute on each side. Press the dough with a towel when it puffs up. Remove the tortilla with your spatula.

This recipe makes about 16 tortillas. These are good with butter or salsa made from tomatoes, garlic, onions, cilantro, and spices.

Darren's Blue Corn Tortillas from the Southwestern United States

You will need a mixing bowl, liquid and dry measuring cups, measuring spoons, a floured breadboard, plastic wrap, a rolling pin, a spatula, and a skillet.

In the mixing bowl, combine:

1-1/2 cups blue cornmeal
1 cup unbleached all-purpose flour
1 teaspoon salt
1 cup warm water

Mix the dough with your hands. Use your hands to roll the dough into 16 walnut-size balls. If your dough seems too soft to easily roll out on the breadboard, press tortillas out between sheets of plastic wrap. Then peel off the plastic wrap and cook these just like the regular corn tortillas recipe in this book.

This recipe makes 16 tortillas and is served with any meal. Have it for breakfast with eggs, at lunch with cheese, or with a dinner of meat or stew.

Darren's Piki, or Indian Paper Bread, from the Pueblo Indians

Kitchen equipment for this recipe includes a mixing bowl, a liquid measuring cup, measuring spoons, a wire whisk, a spatula, and a skillet.

In the mixing bowl, combine:

5 tablespoons masa harina (corn flour)
2 tablespoons cornstarch
1/8 teaspoon salt
1 cup hot water

Whisk the batter until it is smooth.

Carefully pour 1/4 cup of the batter in a circular motion, just barely covering the bottom of the pan. Cook for 1 minute. These breads are only cooked on one side. Peel the tortilla up with your spatula and lay it on a paper towel. Cook 2 more pikis.

When you have cooked 3 pikis, lay them one on top of the other, like a flat sandwich. Then, roll them up together so they resemble a scroll.

Continue to use the rest of the batter, making each scroll consist of 3 pikis.

You will be able to make 8 scrolls of bread with this recipe. They are eaten with salsa and stew.

Melissa's Chinese Pancakes from Beijing

For this recipe, you will need a mixing bowl, liquid and dry measuring cups, measuring spoons, a wooden spoon, a floured breadboard, a rolling pin, a warm towel, a spatula, and a skillet. A pastry brush may be used, but it is optional.

In the mixing bowl, combine:

2-1/2 cups unbleached, all-purpose flour
1 cup hot water
2 tablespoons roasted sesame oil (store this oil in the refrigerator)

Have a little vegetable oil available in a small dish

Stir all of the ingredients (with the exception of the vegetable oil) with the wooden spoon in the bowl. When it is cool enough to touch, knead this dough for 12 minutes, then let it sit in the bowl for at least 15 minutes.

After letting the dough rest, lay the dough on a floured breadboard. Make 12 walnut-size dough balls. Roll them out to about 6 to 7 inches in diameter, which will make them appear very thin. If the dough is sticky, keep flouring your breadboard and rolling pin.

With a pastry brush or soft paper towel, spread a little vegetable oil on the top of 6 of the flatbreads. Lay the remaining 6 pancakes on top of the oiled ones. You will cook them all in pairs.

After cooking for about a minute in the skillet, the cooked side will appear to have freckles. With your spatula, turn the pancakes over to cook for 1 minute more. When cooked, transfer them to a warm towel and gently pull them apart. Wrap them up to keep them warm while you cook the rest of the dough using the same process.

You'll have approximately 12 soft pancakes ready to stuff with your favorite Chinese food.

Melissa's Nan Bread from China

This recipe requires a mixing bowl, liquid and dry measuring cups, measuring spoons, a wooden spoon, a floured breadboard, a rolling pin, a spatula, and a skillet.

In the mixing bowl, combine:

2 teaspoons dry yeast, or 1 packet of dry yeast granules
2-1/2 cups lukewarm water

With your wooden spoon, stir in:
3 cups unbleached white flour

Stir for about 1 minute. Add:
1 tablespoon salt
2-1/2 cups flour

Knead with your hands.

Topping:
¼ teaspoon cumin
¼ cup chopped onions or scallions (baby onions)
¼ teaspoon salt

Place the dough on a floured breadboard and knead for about 8 minutes.

Return the dough to a clean bowl, cover, and let it rise for about 1-1/2 hours.

Return dough to the floured breadboard and divide it into 12–14 pieces. Flatten each piece with your hands until they are about 4-inch rounds. Roll them out to about 8 inches in diameter, cover, and let them rise for ten minutes.

Flatten the center area of each circle again and sprinkle with salt, cumin, and scallions.

Cook on a skillet until each side has freckles (brown spots). They are torn in pieces and wrapped around cooked lamb or chicken, or they can be dipped in tea or plain yogurt. Nan or naan breads have been eaten in Asia for thousands of years. More naan bread recipes follow.

David's Chapatis, Also Called Rotis, from India

Your equipment for this recipe will be a mixing bowl, liquid and dry measuring cups, measuring spoons, a wooden spoon, a floured breadboard, a damp dishtowel, a thick towel (or a folded paper towel), a rolling pin, a spatula, and a skillet.

In the mixing bowl, combine:

2 cups finely ground whole wheat flour
1 teaspoon salt
2 teaspoons vegetable oil
1 cup warm water

After mixing the dough in the bowl with a wooden spoon, knead the dough on the floured board until it is thoroughly mixed. Cover the dough with a damp dishtowel, and let it stand for about 30 minutes.

Form 8 Ping-Pong-size balls of dough, and pat them between your hands. Roll out each one until they become 8-inch rounds.

Lay each circle in a hot skillet and cook for about 1 minute on each side. If the bread bubbles up, press the air out with a thick towel, or a paper towel folded over several times.

These delicious breads are eaten with all Indian food. You can include a side dish of chopped onions, garlic, and tomatoes.

Logan's Naan Bread from India

This recipe requires cooking in an oven. You will need a small mixing bowl, a medium mixing bowl, dry measuring cups, measuring spoons, a wire whisk, a wooden spoon, a floured breadboard, a damp cloth, a spatula, and a pizza stone or cookie sheet.

In the small bowl, whisk together:

1 large egg
2 tablespoons plain yogurt
3 tablespoons milk
1 tablespoon vegetable oil

In the medium bowl, mix:

1-1/2 cups all-purpose flour
1 teaspoon salt
1-1/2 teaspoons baking powder
1 teaspoon sugar

Use the wooden spoon to stir the liquids from the small bowl into the flour mixture in the medium bowl.

Transfer the dough to the floured breadboard. Knead until firm. Place dough into the medium mixing bowl and cover with a damp cloth to rest for at least 2 hours.

Preheat the oven to 350 degrees. Return the dough to the breadboard again, and divide into 4 equal pieces. Knead each piece again and press them out as flat as you can get them; they will be about 7 inches in diameter. (You may need to pull them gently in all directions to get them the right size.)

You can top the naan with chopped onion and Indian spices that can be found in the Indian foods section of grocery stores. Naan are traditionally cooked in an upright *tandoori* oven, but cooking them on a cookie sheet will be fine. Bake for about 5 minutes, or until the bread puffs up and blisters. Carefully remove with a spatula. You may also brush them with melted butter before serving.

Brandon's Fatir Bread, or Bedouin Barley Bread, from Jordan

You will need a mixing bowl, liquid and dry measuring cups, measuring spoons, a wooden spoon, a floured breadboard, a rolling pin, a thick cloth or towel, a spatula, and a skillet or a wok. A wok is a bowl-shaped pan that is used in Chinese culture to cook stir-fry meals on the stove.

In the mixing bowl, combine:

1 cup barley flour
1 cup unbleached white flour
1 teaspoon salt
1 cup warm water

After mixing the dough with the wooden spoon, use your hands to mix the dough. Turn it out on to a floured breadboard and form 8 golf-ball-size pieces. Roll them out on the floured breadboard to about 8 inches in diameter.

These pieces can be cooked in a skillet, about 1 minute on each side. Turn them with your spatula and press them with a thick cloth or towel to keep them flat.

Brandon makes yogurt cheese balls (a mixture of plain yogurt, cream cheese and salt) to have with this bread.

You can also have fun and cook them like they are done in Jordan. There, they are cooked on a large, metal bowl called a *sajj*, which looks like an upside-down wok. Woks are bowl-shaped skillets that are used by the Chinese to quickly cook their food over high heat. The bowl-shaped bottom part of the wok sits inside the round burners of the stove top. When the wok is turned over and heated, the top and sides provide a large hot surface on which to cook flatbreads.

Brandon's Fenugreek Corn Bread from Egypt

You will need a large size mixing bowl, liquid and dry measuring cups, measuring spoons, a rolling pin, a wooden spoon, a floured breadboard, a paper towel, a clean towel, a spatula, and a skillet. Try to get a friend to help you with this one. You'll have fun!

In a large bowl, pour:

1-1/2 cups lukewarm water
Sprinkle in and stir:
1 teaspoon dry yeast
2 tablespoons packed brown sugar
Add 1-1/2 cups unbleached white flour
1 teaspoon salt
1 teaspoon fenugreek powder (found in the Indian spice section of the supermarket)
1-1/2 cups corn flour (Mexican masa flour also works well)

You will also need a small amount of oil set aside.

After the ingredients are thoroughly mixed, turn the dough onto a floured breadboard and knead for 5 minutes. Rinse the mixing bowl, and then use a paper towel to spread a little oil in the clean bowl.

Place the dough back in the bowl and cover it with a clean towel to keep it free from wind and dust. Let it rise for 1-1/2 hours.

Punch down the dough and let it sit for 5 more minutes. Return it to the floured breadboard. Divide the dough into about 8 Ping-Pong-size balls. Roll them out into 7-inch circles. Let circles rise again for 20 minutes.

Cook the dough in a skillet for 1 minute on each side, or until you see freckles. Carefully remove the bread with your spatula, and place them on a plate. Cover them with a towel to keep them warm.

Wrap the bread around a mixture of chopped kalamata olives, tomatoes, and hot sauce.

Tina's Lavash from Armenia

Lavash is cooked the same way as Brandon's Bedouin Barley Bread. You will need a mixing bowl, liquid and dry measuring cups, measuring spoons, a wooden spoon, a floured breadboard, a rolling pin, a spatula, vegetable oil, and a wok. If you don't have a wok, just use a skillet.

In the mixing bowl, combine:

3/4 cup lukewarm water
1/2 tablespoon honey
1/2 teaspoon dry yeast
Gradually stir in:
1 cup unbleached white flour
1/2 teaspoon salt
1 more cup flour

Mix with your wooden spoon until the dough begins to form a ball. Turn the dough out onto a floured breadboard and knead for 8 minutes.

Return the dough to a clean bowl, cover, and let it sit for 3 hours. Punch down the dough and let it rise again for 10 minutes.

Divide the dough into 8 golf-ball-size pieces. Roll out the pieces to about 7 inches in diameter. You may need to stretch them back to the 7-inch size before cooking. Turn the wok upside down over the burner (or use your skillet, right side up). These breads are cooked just as Brandon's Fatir Bread from Jordan is cooked. Please read that recipe for an explanation of the wok. Cook the bread for 30 seconds or until you see freckles, then turn it with your spatula to the other side. Cook it for 40 seconds, or until done.

Lavash is wrapped around meat chunks that have been cooked on skewers.

Suzanne's Oasis Bread from Tunisia

This recipe requires a mixing bowl, liquid and dry measuring cups, measuring spoons, a wooden spoon, a floured breadboard, a rolling pin, a spatula, and a skillet.

In the mixing bowl, combine:

3 cups unbleached all-purpose flour
1 cup unbleached white flour
2 teaspoons salt
2 cups warm water
Optional filling:
1 cup Mexican salsa, strained

Knead the dough consisting of the first four ingredients until everything is mixed together, cover, and set aside for 30 minutes.

Divide the dough into eight balls. On a floured breadboard, roll out each ball to about 7 inches in diameter. Traditionally, they are filled before cooking with 1 tablespoon of a delicious mixture of scallions, tomatoes, and spices. This spice mixture tastes very much like the Mexican salsa available in jars at the grocery store.

To fill each circle of dough with salsa, first divide your 8 balls of dough into 16 balls. Roll out the dough into circles, top 8 of them with strained salsa, then lay another flattened pancake on top and seal the edges with moistened fingers. Cook on a skillet for 1 minute on each side, turning them with your spatula.

This recipe makes 8 savory flatbreads with a wonderful stuffing inside!

Jason's Piadine from Italy

You will need a mixing bowl, liquid and dry measuring cups, measuring spoons, a floured breadboard, a clean towel, a rolling pin, a fork, a spatula, and a skillet.

In the mixing bowl, combine:

1-3/4 cups sifted unbleached all-purpose white flour
1/2 teaspoon baking powder
1/2 teaspoon salt

Make a well in the center of the flour mixture with your fingers.
Pour 1/4 cup extra virgin olive oil in the center.
Mix with your fingers as you add:
1/2 cup warm water

Mix the dough with your fingers. Turn the dough onto the floured breadboard and knead for about 5 minutes.

Clean the bowl and oil it lightly. Place the bread dough back in the bowl and cover with a clean kitchen towel for 20 minutes. Divide the dough into 8 Ping-Pong-size balls. Roll each one out to about 7 inches in diameter.

Cook on a hot skillet for 1 minute on the first side. Use the spatula to turn them over and cook 1 to 1-1/2 minutes on the other side. You may prick the tops with a fork to prevent bubbles from forming, or press out the bubbles with a towel or spatula as they are cooking.

These breads are delicious with Italian soups and dips. They can also be stuffed with chopped and seasoned Italian vegetables, or folded over ham and cheese and heated in a skillet.

Jason's Injera from Ethiopia

For this recipe, gather together a large mixing bowl, liquid and dry measuring cups, measuring spoons, a wire whisk, and a nonstick skillet with cover.

In the bowl, mix:

3 cups all-purpose flour
3 teaspoons baking powder
1-1/2 teaspoons salt

Stir in:
2 eggs beaten
3 cups club soda

Whisk the batter until it resembles pancake batter. Heat the skillet to medium-high. When it is hot, pour 1/2 cup of the batter in the pan, tipping your skillet to coat the entire bottom to form a large pancake.

Cover and let it cook for 2–3 minutes. The pancake will appear shiny and bubbly. Only one side of the pancake needs to be cooked in the skillet. Lift the pancake off the pan with the spatula and lay it on a plate to cool. Repeat this process for each bread.

This recipe makes 10 breads about 8 inches in diameter. Tear off pieces and wrap around spicy chicken or beef. These breads are often placed on a dinner plate and a meat stew poured on the top. Then, pieces are torn from another *injera* to use as a scoop to eat the stew.

Dylan's Lefse, or Wrapping Bread, from Norway

You will need a mixing bowl, liquid and dry measuring cups, measuring spoons, a wooden spoon, a floured breadboard, a rolling pin, a spatula, and a skillet.

In the mixing bowl, combine all of these ingredients:

2 cups mashed potatoes (prepared instant mashed potatoes work well)
2 cups unbleached all-purpose flour
1/3 cup soft unsalted butter
1 cup heavy cream
1-1/2 teaspoons salt

Knead the dough on a floured surface. You may even let it sit covered in a bowl in a refrigerator overnight. Pull off 12 golf-ball-size dough balls, and roll them out to 7-inch-round circles.

Cook on a hot skillet for about 1 minute on each side, turning with your spatula.

Lefse are served topped with sugar and jam for breakfast, or wrapped around meat or cheese for a delicious snack.

Dylan's Lumpe from Norway

These are very much like *lefse*, but are smaller and thicker. You will need a mixing bowl, liquid and dry measuring cups, measuring spoons, a wooden spoon, a floured breadboard, a rolling pin, a spatula, and a skillet.

In the mixing bowl, combine:

2 cups prepared mashed potatoes (instant potatoes work well)
1 cup barley flour
1 cup unbleached all-purpose flour
1 teaspoon salt

Knead the dough on the floured breadboard for about 3 minutes, and then divide the dough into twelve golf-ball-size sections. Press each section into a thick circle. Roll out the circle into 5-inch-diameter rounds.

Cook in your skillet for about 1 minute on each side, and use a fork to prick any blisters that form while it is cooking to release the air from the bubbles. When you see large brown freckles, you know they are done.

Lumpe is eaten with butter and sugar on top or wrapped around sharp goat cheese. They are most often served with spicy sausage and mustard.

Vanessa's Pita Bread from Greece

This recipe requires a mixing bowl, liquid and dry measuring cups, measuring spoons, a wooden spoon, a floured breadboard, a rolling pin, a towel, a spatula, and a skillet.

In the mixing bowl, combine:

1 teaspoon dry yeast
1-1/4 cups lukewarm water
Slowly stir in:
1-1/2 cups whole wheat flour
Stir for about 1 minute.
Cover and let this mixture sit for at least 10 minutes.
Stir in:
1/2 tablespoon salt
1/2 tablespoon olive oil
Mix in:
1-1/2 more cups unbleached white flour

Knead this dough for 10 minutes on a floured breadboard. Return it to a clean bowl, cover, and let sit for 1-1/2 hours.

Gently punch down the dough and divide into 8 balls. Roll these out to 8 inches in diameter.

Cook the rounds on a skillet for 45 seconds, turn over with your spatula, and cook for 1 more minute. Turn the bread back to the first side until it's done. Use a towel to press out the bubbles that form during cooking.

Pita bread is eaten with all meals, including rice, salads, and meats. You may wrap the bread around your food, or you can cut the bread in half and gently separate the top and bottom halves to form a pouch. Spoon your food inside for a great sandwich!

Carisa's Pebbled Persian Nan Bread from Iran

You will need a mixing bowl, liquid and dry measuring cups, measuring spoons, a wooden spoon, plastic wrap, a floured breadboard, a spatula, and a skillet.

In the mixing bowl, combine:

1-1/2 cups warm water
2 teaspoons dry yeast (1 package)
Sprinkle in:
3 cups whole wheat flour
1 teaspoon salt
1 teaspoon vegetable oil

Mix with the wooden spoon until the dough begins to form a ball. Turn the dough onto the floured breadboard and knead for 8 minutes, wetting your hands with water if needed. Return the dough to an oiled bowl, cover, and let it rise for 1-1/2 hours.

Punch down the dough. Cover and let rise for another 30 minutes. Cover the breadboard with a large piece of plastic wrap, and sprinkle it with a handful of water. This will keep your working surface moist so that the bread doesn't stick.

Gently punch down the dough again, and then divide it into 10 equal dough balls, each about the size of a golf ball. Pat each ball flat with wet fingers. Lay your flattened dough on your wet surface, and keep pressing dough out until it is 6 inches around.

Cook on an oiled skillet for 2 minutes. Turn over and cook for 2 more minutes.

The bread will have a pebbled appearance and is delicious with any Persian food.

Erin's Rice Paper Wraps from Vietnam

This recipe requires 2 large bowls, liquid and dry measuring cups, measuring spoons, a wire whisk, a sieve, a small skillet with a tight-fitting lid, a baking sheet, a large plate, a tablespoon, and a wooden spatula.

In the mixing bowl, combine:

1/2 cup rice flour
1/2 cup cornstarch
1/2 cup tapioca flour or potato starch
1-1/4 cups water
1 tablespoon vegetable oil
(Have 1/4 cup of extra oil ready)

Whisk until batter is smooth. Strain the batter through a sieve into the second mixing bowl, pressing out the lumps. Let it sit in the bowl for 30 minutes.

Oil the skillet and heat it to medium high. Whisk the batter again, and pour 1/4 cup of batter onto the hot skillet, lifting the handle of the skillet in different directions to swirl the batter around to coat the bottom of the skillet. Cover with the lid and let it cook for 1 minute. When the rice sheet appears shiny, remove it with the spatula to cool down on an oiled baking sheet.

Before you make the next one, wipe excess moisture off the lid for the skillet. Continue making the wraps until the batter is gone.

This recipe makes about 16–18 rice papers that are 7–8 inches across. These papers can often be purchased in a Vietnamese market. They are called *banh trang,* and they are purchased dry. They are dipped in a bowl of water for just a few seconds to make them pliable. These bland breads are perfect to wrap around spicy fish or meat, and they can be dipped in a chili or peanut sauce.

Genevieve's Lumpia Wrappers from the Philippines

You will need a mixing bowl, a wire whisk, a skillet, a 4-cup (quart-size) measuring cup, a spatula, a skillet, a towel, and a plate.

In the mixing bowl, beat together:

2 eggs plus 2 egg whites
1 cup flour
1 cup cornstarch
Add:
1 teaspoon salt
3 cups water

Whisk the mixture until it is smooth.

Oil the skillet and heat on medium high heat until a drop of water spatters on it. Pour 1/2 cup of batter around the skillet bottom and swirl batter until the bottom of pan is coated. Cook for 2 minutes, and then flip the crepe to the other side with your spatula. Cook for 1-1/2 more minutes.

Remove to a towel on a plate to keep them moist and warm. This recipe makes 14 wrappers.

To eat, first place a lettuce leaf on top of the wrapper. This keeps moisture from the food. Next, fill with 1/3 cup spicy meat and vegetables. Wrap carefully and enjoy.

Seth's Matzo Bread from Israel

You will need a mixing bowl, liquid and dry measuring cups, measuring spoons, a wooden spoon, a rolling pin, a floured breadboard, a spatula, a fork, and a skillet.

In the mixing bowl, mix together:

2 cups whole wheat flour
1 teaspoon salt
1 tablespoon olive oil
1 cup water

Turn the dough out onto a floured breadboard and knead quickly for 3–4 minutes. Divide the dough into 12 pieces, and flatten each one with your hands.

Roll out each piece as thinly as possible, prick all over with the fork and stretch the bread out again. (Pricking with a fork prevents them from rising as they cook and is a very important part of the traditional recipe.) The dough should be about 8–10 inches in diameter.

Cook the pieces on a skillet for 1 minute on each side, carefully turning them over with your spatula.

The bread is delicious with a sauce of plain yogurt mixed with tahini (a bean spread found in most supermarkets). Matzo is eaten as warm, moist breads, or it can be dried and eaten as crackers.

Seth's Spelt Breakfast Bread from Switzerland

You will need a mixing bowl, liquid and dry measuring cups, measuring spoons, a wooden spoon, a floured breadboard, a rolling pin, a spatula, and a skillet.

In the mixing bowl, combine:

1 cup warm water
2 tablespoons olive oil
2 tablespoons honey
1 teaspoon salt

Stir in:
1-1/2 cups all-purpose flour
1-1/2 cups spelt flour

Knead the dough on a floured breadboard for about 5 minutes. Cover and let sit for about 10 minutes.

Divide the dough into 12 Ping-Pong-size balls. Flatten each ball into 3-inch-round disks with your hands, and then roll them out on the breadboard with a rolling pin.

Cook them on a heated skillet for about 1 minute on each side. Serve them warm with honey or marmalade.

References

Alford, Jeffrey and Naomi Duguid. *Flatbreads and Flavors; a Baker's Atlas*. New York: William Morrow & Co., Inc., 1995.

Brown, Ellen. *Southwest Tastes*. Hong Kong: Great Chefs Publishing, 1990.

Dent, Huntley. *The Feast of Santa Fe; Cooking of the American West*. New York: Simon and Schuster, 1985.

Finger Food Feast. Sunset Publishing Corporation, March 2006.

Ingram, Christine and Jennie Shapter. *The Cook's Encyclopedia of Bread*. New York: Barnes & Noble Books, 2000.

Kennedy, Diana. *The Tortilla Book*. New York: Harper & Row Publishers, 1975.

Rombauer, Irma and Marion Rombauer Becker. *The Joy of Cooking*. Toronto: The Bobbs-Merrill Co., Inc., 1967.

Wilbur, Todd. *Top Secret Restaurant Recipes*. New York: The Penguin Group, 1997.

www.cooking.com

www.epicurious.com

www.foodtv.com

www.gonorway.com

www.recipesource.com

www.touregypt.net

Many thanks to the following wonderful cooks for their contributions:

Tina Real for her time-tested flour tortilla recipe

Josie Gomes for her *Lumpia* recipe

Asheesh & Bindu Danee for their *Chapati* recipe

Laura Ogles for her *Lefse* recipe

"Dolly has brought her love of children and cooking together into an inspiring story and cookbook for families. This book will help children of all ages to appreciate their heritage and to learn to love cooking."

—Carolyn Murphy, mother and international model and actress

978-0-595-39001-‹
0-595-39001-3

Printed in the United States
60700LVS00005B/85-111

9 780595 390014